NEW CRAFTS
PAPERMAKING

NEW CRAFTS

PAPERMAKING

25 creative handmade projects shown step by step

ELIZABETH COUZINS-SCOTT

PHOTOGRAPHY BY PETER WILLIAMS

LORENZ BOOKS

This edition is published by Lorenz Books,
an imprint of Anness Publishing Ltd,
108 Great Russell Street,
London WC1B 3NA;
info@anness.com

www.lorenzbooks.com;
www.annesspublishing.com

If you like the images in this book and would like to investigate
using them for publishing, promotions or advertising, please visit
our website www.practicalpictures.com for more information.

© Anness Publishing Ltd 2014

A CIP catalogue record for this book
is available from the British Library.

Publisher: Joanna Lorenz
Project Editors: Emma Clegg and Felicity Forster
Photographer: Peter Williams
Step Photographer: Rodney Forte
Stylist: Georgina Rhodes
Illustrators: Madeleine David and Rob Highton
Designers: Lilian Lindblom and Lucy Doncaster
Production Controller: Mai-Ling Collyer

PUBLISHER'S NOTE
Although the advice and information in this book are believed to be
accurate and true at the time of going to press, neither the authors
nor the publisher can accept any legal responsibility or liability
for any errors or omissions that may have been made nor for any
inaccuracies nor for any loss, harm or injury that comes about from
following instructions or advice in this book.

Bracketed terms are intended for American readers.

PICTURE CREDITS
Thank you to the following agencies and museums for permission
to reproduce pictures in this book: page 8, British Museum,
London/Bridgeman Art Library, London/New York (top),
Bibliotheque Nationale, Tunis/Lauros-Giraudon/Bridgeman Art
Library, London/New York (bottom); page 9, ET Archive (top);
Oriental Museum, Durham University/Bridgeman Art Library,
London/New York (bottom left); Jacqui Hurst Picture Library
(bottom right).

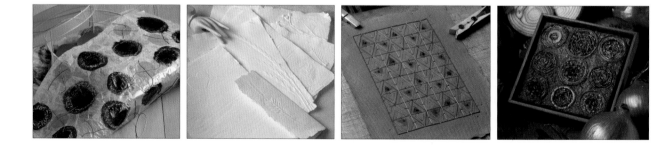

Contents

INTRODUCTION

Although paper is mass-produced industrially, papermaking is an ancient handmade craft now increasingly adopted by contemporary artists.

Producing your own sheet of paper is incredibly satisfying. During the making process, paper pulp can be dyed, shaped into bowls and embossed or cast over interesting shapes. Delicate tissue paper can be laminated to produce a strong, translucent surface, and petals, leaves and grasses can be embedded in the pulp while it is still wet. Finished handmade paper can be decorated with embroidery or paints and inks.

The 25 projects in this book, each explained with step-by-step instructions, show how you can combine these techniques to make highly individual and achievable designs. This, combined with inspiring examples of contemporary work in the gallery section, will give you a rich array of ideas and techniques with which to make your own personal paper creations.

Opposite: A wide range of textures, colours and finishes can be achieved when making paper at home.

HISTORY OF PAPERMAKING

Papermaking has a long and fascinating history, but for centuries the technique, discovered in China, was a well-hidden secret. Once introduced to the West, papermaking was developed to suit European styles of writing and later, printing. In recent years artists and craftspeople have become increasingly interested in the rich qualities of handmade paper and have looked back to its historical roots for inspiration.

The word 'paper' is derived from the papyrus used in Ancient Egypt, although the technique used then was quite different from those employed in modern papermaking. The stems of the papyrus plant, which grew abundantly by the banks of the River Nile, were cut and split, then laid at right angles to each other like a woven mat of reeds. This was wetted with muddy water from the Nile, then pounded together to form a hard, thin sheet and left to dry in the sun. Perfectly preserved documents dating from 3500BC have been discovered in the tombs of the Pharaohs, and the works of Greek and Roman scholars were also written on papyrus.

The earliest evidence of papermaking as we know it has been traced to China in about AD105. Its inventor, Ts'ai Lun, was searching for an alternative writing medium to replace the carved strips of bamboo or silk then in use. He experimented with various materials, including old rags, fishing nets and plants such as hemp and mulberry. He also discovered that macerating and beating these materials produced a substance that could be suspended in water and collected on a woven fabric stretched across a frame. The matted material was left to dry in the sun to form a sheet of paper. Ts'ai Lun was rewarded for his pains by being imprisoned so that the Chinese government could keep the secret of papermaking to themselves and he eventually committed suicide.

China kept his invention hidden for over 600 years until the Arabs conquered Samarkand in the 8th century. Ts'ai Lun's technique spread through the trade routes, reaching Central Asia by AD751 and Baghdad by AD793. It reached Japan through Buddhist monks, who carried books made of mulberry leaf paper, and developed into a very refined activity and an essential part of Japanese culture.

Historians believe that the Moorish invasion of Spain brought papermakers to Europe. The first recorded paper mill was established in Cordoba in 1036, over 900 years after Ts'ai Lun's original discovery. From Spain, papermaking spread throughout Europe and the technique was improved in Germany, which produced

Above: The Book of the Dead of the Scribe Ani, 19th Dynasty, c.1250BC, British Museum, London, was beautifully painted on papyrus.

Below: This page from the Koran, 9th century, Bibliothèque Nationale, Tunis, was painted on vellum – a parchment made from calf skin.

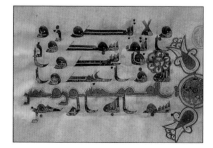

Above: Print showing the traditional process of couching and pressing sheets adopted in Chinese papermaking.

the finest papers at that time. With Johann Gutenberg's invention of the printing press in 1453, the demand for books, and therefore paper, greatly increased.

Oriental papers were made from plant fibres, producing a soft, flexible paper, ideal for Chinese calligraphy. A tougher paper was needed in Europe, where writers used sharp quill pens. The idea of making paper from old clothes, cotton rags and linen was introduced, as was sealing the surface with a gelatine solution to give a non-absorbent surface. Paper mills were located near a supply of flowing water, used in the production of the pulp and as an energy source.

Initially the materials were beaten by hand but this was replaced by a stamping machine, with heavy hammers moving up and down continually to break up the fibres. In 1680 the Dutch invented the Hollander Beating Machine, which consisted of a large tub with a revolving roller which chopped, pounded and pulverized the rags against a stone plate. This greatly shortened the time required to reduce rags to pulp and was a major step forward.

By 1719 the demand for paper was so great that there was a critical shortage of cotton and linen rags. Réné Antoine Ferchault de Reamur, a French naturalist who had studied wasps building their nests, thought that it was possible to grind wood fine enough to produce cellulose for papermaking. Refined wood pulp, to which chemicals are added, is used for industrially produced paper to this day.

The final step to revolutionize industrial papermaking was a continuous rotating machine invented in 1798 by an Englishman, Nicholas Robert. It was perfected by the Fourdrinier brothers in 1806 and, even though they did not use their invention, all papermaking machines bear their name. They produced rolls of paper, replacing the hand-papermaker's craft and making the industry into the highly mechanized process it is today.

Making paper by hand remains a similar process to that used by the early craftspeople. Most professional hand-papermakers use prepared fibres called cotton linters, which are cotton lengths too short for spinning into cloth. The fibres are beaten until they intertwine, or 'felt', when shaken by the 'vatman', who then dips a mould and deckle into the vat of pulp. The mould is a hardwood frame with crossbars at intervals to which a fine wire screen is sewn. The deckle, a similar frame but without the screen, stops the pulp from running off the mould.

The mould is then passed to the 'coucher', who presses the sheets face downward, sandwiching each between white wool felts. Pressure is applied to remove the water, then the sheets are separated and hung or laid out to dry naturally for 4–5 days. The sheets are then sized and left to settle. The best handmade papers are thus free from any additives.

Above: This seven-sided kite depicting a warrior is made from paper and bamboo, Japanese, 20th century, Oriental Museum, Durham University, England.

Above: The continuing tradition of papermaking; hanging up pieces of paper to dry at the Two Rivers Paper Company, Somerset, England.

GALLERY

Papermaking is a tremendously versatile craft. As well as allowing us to create beautiful textured surfaces for writing paper, wrapping paper or just for framing, there is also an abundance of ways to decorate and embellish the surfaces during or after the papermaking process, and to manipulate it to create more three-dimensional work. This glimpse of the work of contemporary papermakers reflects the astonishing possibilities of what can be achieved with this ancient craft and its core materials of water and recycled pulp.

Left: HOARD 10–30cm (4–12in) diameter. A series of paper vessels made from hand-beaten Kozo paper, which incorporate knitted copper wire, cotton scrims, paper yarn and unbeaten plant fibres. The pieces were inspired by research into Ancient Roman archaeological sites. Anne Johnson

Below: WISH YOU WERE HERE 175 x 114cm (69 x 45in) This piece was made with cotton linters, using small paper pieces laminated together while the pieces were wet. Washes of acrylic and wax were then added, creating a rich and painterly effect. Carol Farrow

Right: PAPER QUILT
140 x 192cm
(55 x 75in)
This paper quilt was made from recycled, dyed paper pulp, working on a nine-square block. The piece was made by amateurs at a drop-in workshop run by paper artist Anne Johnson at the Shipley Art Gallery (Gateshead, England) in conjunction with an exhibition of contemporary quilts.
Anne Johnson

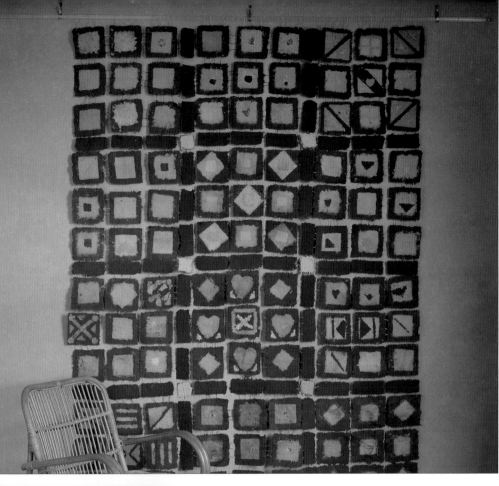

Left: ARROW CHANDELIER
80 x 100 x 100cm
(31½ x 39½ x 39½in)
Dramatic lighting is a powerful way of enhancing large public spaces. This chandelier directs light upwards, creating a warm, ambient environment. The piece is made from laminated paper and fabric folded into sculptural forms, and is compatible with compact fluorescent and tungsten bulbs.
Lindsay Bloxam

Above: ISHTAR
48 x 61cm
(19 x 24in)
This piece combines different casting techniques with decorative surface treatments. Ishtar is an ancient goddess of love and war, and the piece is abstracted to suggest strength and sexuality. The underwear may also represent armour.
Elizabeth Couzins-Scott

Right: STILETTO
Detail of 100 pairs of stiletto shoes in adult sizes. Abaca pulp is made into thin sheets of paper which are then layered, while in wet sheet form, on to a shoe mould. Glue and armatures are not used in the finished pieces.
Susan Cutts

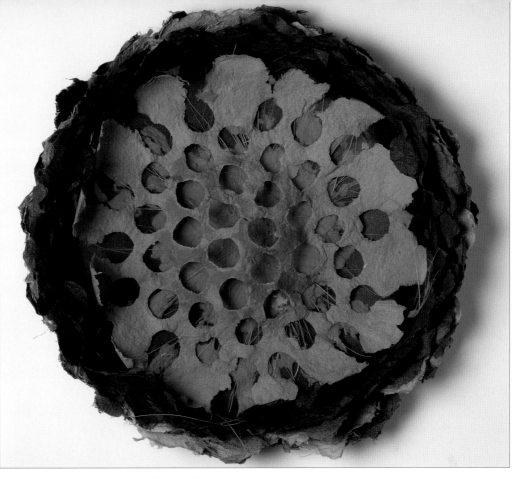

Right: FLEUR DU MAL
45 x 45cm (18 x 18in)
Incorporating dyed cotton linters, plant fibres and horse hair, this form was created by tearing, shaping and casting sheets of paper while wet. Once dry, the paper is removed from the armature. Part of a series exploring the affinity between seeds and flowers and elements of the human anatomy, such as nerve and blood cells.
Wendy Carlton-Dewhirst

Left: STRATA (detail) 520 x 120cm (205 x 47in)
Inspired by layers of rock strata, this paper is made from recycled brown craft paper poured as a very thin pulp on to a large 520cm (205in) screen. This piece is a combination of many sheets built up in layers. The various colour shades were obtained by adding pulped coloured paper to the main pulp stock.
David Watson

MATERIALS

Handmade paper can be made out of many different kinds of scrap paper or plants, so the materials you need are easy to find and very inexpensive. The idea of recycling waste paper appeals to many modern artists and craftspeople, and it is simple to add character and texture with flower petals, leaves, threads or scraps of fabric.

Discarded paper Suitable papers for recycling are computer paper, photocopy paper, shredded paper, brown parcel paper, cartridge (white construction) paper, tissue paper, writing paper, old envelopes and good-quality watercolour paper. The final quality of the recycled sheets will depend on the original paper. Experiment by combining different papers. Newspaper can be used, but it is poor-quality and prone to discolour and break down due to its high acid content; the newsprint will also affect the colour. Glossy magazine paper and papers with shiny surfaces are difficult to recycle because they are chemically treated.

Cotton linters These are plant fibres that have already been partly processed. They come in sheet form and can be purchased from specialist suppliers. Use them to make a basic white pulp or add them to recycled paper pulp to give extra strength.

Rags Paper can be made from cotton and linen rags because of their high cellulose content. Long-lasting linen papers are still used to make paper currency today. Old linen or cotton dish towels, tablecloths, shirts and handkerchiefs are suitable, especially if well-worn. It is necessary to add chemicals to break down the fibres before liquidizing them into pulp.

Extra decorative materials A range of small materials can be added to the basic pulp to add interest. Experiment with torn scraps of other paper (such as glossy paper and newspaper), short lengths of wool (yarn) or thread, flower petals, dried leaves, and scraps of lace or fabric.

Kaolin (ballclay/batwash) clay Added to the vat of pulp, this type of clay helps to give the paper a shiny surface on which to write.

Glues and size If to be used for writing or painting, the recycled sheets of paper should be made less absorbent by adding size to the vat when forming the sheets, or afterwards when they are dry. Suitable products are PVA (white) glue, household starch, gelatine, agar-agar (a gelatine made from seaweed, available from health food shops) or cold-water (wallpaper) paste.

Paints and dyes Any water-based paints, such as powder colours, inks and watercolour, can be added to the liquidized pulp before adding it to the vat. Paper pulp can also be coloured with cold- or hot-water dyes. When dyeing you should protect your surface with a plastic sheet and wear rubber gloves and an apron. If you are mixing dye powder, wear a face mask (respirator) to prevent inhalation of the fine powder.

The surface of the paper can also be decorated after sizing by using any artist's materials, for example acrylic paints, pastels or coloured pencils.

Plants It is possible to make pulp entirely from plant fibres, or you can add them to recycled paper pulp. First soften the fibres and release the cellulose by placing them in a large, heavy pan and boiling the plants in water, with the addition of an alkaline solution such as wood ash, soda ash (anhydrous sodium carbonate) or washing soda (sodium carbonate). Boiling time will vary with different plants, and if after 2–3 hours the material is still not soft, it can be rinsed and reboiled in a fresh solution. For tougher, woody plants, caustic soda (lye or sodium hydroxide) will be necessary. When working with chemicals such as these, ensure that you start by following a recipe with associated safety instructions. Always work in a well-ventilated room when using chemicals and wear rubber gloves and plastic goggles to protect your hands and face.

Different plants produce papers of great individuality and character, with a wide variety of colours and textures. Suitable plants include wild flowers, straw, seaweed, potato, cabbage leaves, leeks, daffodils and nettles.

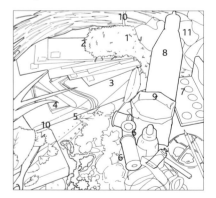

Key
1 Shredded paper
2 Old envelopes
3 Tissue paper
4 Brown paper
5 Computer paper
6 Decorative materials
7 Paints and dyes
8 PVA (white) glue
9 Wallpaper paste
10 Plant materials
11 Cotton dish towel

EQUIPMENT

Creating handmade papers at home requires very little specialist equipment apart from the mould and deckle, and this you can make yourself. The other equipment you need can easily be obtained or adapted from items in daily domestic use.

Bowls and buckets Soak the torn paper scraps in a plastic bowl or bucket to help break down the fibres. It may be necessary to keep different pulps in separate bowls. Also useful for draining pulp for drying or adding colour to the pulp.

Brushes A range of brush sizes is useful for applying paint.

Couching cloths or felts These hold each sheet of pulp after it is lifted out of the vat, and absorb some of the water. Traditionally a pure white wool felt was used, but vilene or smooth disposable dish towels make a good substitute. The first sheet of paper is 'couched' on to a curved surface known as a 'couching mound' made from these folded cloths or newspaper. When making a 'post' of papers (several sheets couched on top of each other), ensure that a felt is placed between each sheet.

Drying board A smooth surface such as Perspex (Plexiglas ®) or formica is useful for drying out the formed sheets of paper evenly and will make the paper smooth.

Iron To obtain a smooth, even surface, iron the sheets of paper while still damp. Iron over a dish towel and then carefully peel the sheet off the cloth.

Liquidizer After soaking, paper is made into pulp by beating the torn scraps to break down the fibres, using an electric liquidizer or blender. Start by mixing a small handful of torn paper with the liquidizer two-thirds full of water, otherwise it may overheat.

Measuring jug (cup) Used to measure how much water to add, to dilute glues and size, and to measure any chemicals.

Mould and deckle This essential piece of equipment can be purchased from specialist suppliers, or you can easily make your own (see Basic Techniques). The mould is a wooden frame across which a layer of mesh is stretched; the deckle is another frame the same size but without the mesh. Any robust, flat-sided picture frames would serve the purpose.

Net Curtaining, silk-screen fabric, aluminium mesh from car accessory suppliers or fibreglass window screening can be used for the mesh as long as it is tautly stretched across the frame. You can also experiment with different fabrics and plastic garden nets to create interesting surfaces.

Sieve (strainer) A sieve is very useful for draining pulp to make it thicker or for drying pulp to use later. Do not pour pulp down the sink as it may block the drain.

Newspaper Used for absorbing water during pressing and can be used to make a couching mound (see Basic Techniques).

Pressing boards Once a 'post' of papers is completed, the sheets are pressed between boards to remove as much water as possible and help the fibres to bond. Make your own pressing boards out of plywood, sealed with two coats of acrylic varnish. The boards should be larger than the sheets of paper. Some papermakers stand on the boards, others use bricks as weights or g-clamps to press the boards together.

Protective equipment It is important to wear rubber gloves and plastic goggles or a face mask (respirator) when handling chemicals such as caustic soda or dyes.

Stainless steel or enamel pan This is needed to boil plant material. Do not use aluminium as it will react with the alkaline solution used to break down the plant fibres and damage the pan. A larger pan is generally better.

Vat The vat can be any rectangular-shaped plastic container, large enough to accommodate the mould and deckle – a large plastic bowl or plastic storage box would be suitable. The pulp is added to clean water in the vat and the mould and deckle are dipped into the pulp to lift a sheet out.

Wide waterproof adhesive tape (duct tape) If you plan to make up a mould and deckle, this will secure the mesh to the mould.

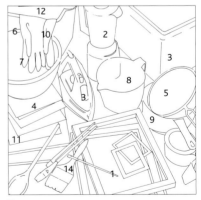

Key

1 Mould and deckle
2 Liquidizer
3 Vat
4 Dish towels
5 Sieve (strainer)
6 Bucket
7 Bowl
8 Measuring jug (cup)
9 Stainless steel pan
10 Rubber gloves
11 Pressing boards
12 Plastic board
13 Iron
14 Brushes

BASIC TECHNIQUES

The techniques of making handmade paper are very simple to learn, and the more you practise, the more skilled and professional the finished results will be. Mastering the following basic techniques will enable you to complete all of the projects in this book, and create your own unique designs.

MAKING A MOULD AND DECKLE

Mould and deckles are easily available and it is also possible to improvise with existing frames by adding an aluminium mesh. However, if you need one at an exact size, the construction method is really very simple.

1 For the mould, cut four pieces of wood to the paper size you require, checking that the dimensions will fit comfortably inside your vat. Lay them on a flat surface and glue together at the corners with waterproof glue. When dry, drill holes in each corner for L-shaped brackets.

2 Screw an L-shaped bracket to each corner of the mould.

3 Cut aluminium (or other) mesh to size and stretch it very tightly across the mould. Attach it with staples or nails.

4 Place strips of thick, wide, waterproof adhesive tape (duct tape) over the stapled or nailed edges to secure the mesh completely. Repeat steps 1–2 to make the deckle. Varnish the mould and deckle before use.

THE PAPERMAKING PROCESS

There are several stages to the craft of papermaking – preparing the pulp and vat, making a sheet of paper, couching it and finally pressing and drying.

Preparing the pulp

Pulp can be prepared immediately before papermaking, or alternatively it can be dried and stored for future use. Note that when selecting paper to use for the pulp, the colour of the original paper will always affect the sheets.

1 Tear the paper into postage-stamp-sized pieces. Use 12–15 sheets of A4 (8½ x 11in) paper to experiment with. Soak the paper scraps for at least 2 hours.

2 Place a small handful of torn paper in a liquidizer and fill it two-thirds with water. Liquidize for short periods only (10–15 seconds) until the paper is broken down into pulp.

3 Pour the pulp through a sieve (strainer). Excess pulp can be dried and saved, or added to the pulp you are using if you want to make it thicker.

4 If you wish to colour the paper, add dye or water-based paint at this stage, when the pulp is thick.

5 To dry pulp for later use, pour it through a cloth with a sieve and bowl underneath. Do not pour pulp down the sink as it may block the drain.

6 Remove all excess water by rolling the cloth round the pulp and then squeeze it. The dried pulp can then be stored in an airtight container. To re-use, just dissolve the dried pulp in water.

Preparing the vat and couching mound

Prepare the vat and couching mound to your satisfaction before starting to make paper sheets. This is because it is necessary to work quickly and confidently as soon as you have started to draw the first sheet.

1 Pour about 3–5 litres (5–9 pints) of clean water into a plastic bowl that is big enough to accommodate the mould and deckle easily. Add the prepared pulp, until the pulp and water mixture is the consistency of soup. For a first attempt, start with 1 litre (2 pints) of pulp. To make thick sheets of paper, add more pulp; if the sheets are too thick, add more water.

2 Extra decorative materials, such as flower petals or threads, can be added to the vat now or later. This is also the time to add any prepared plant fibres.

3 A slightly curved couching mound will make it easier to transfer the pulp sheet. First make two pressing boards, reserving one for later use (see Equipment) and cover with some sheets of newspaper. Fold three smooth cloths into small, medium and large shapes to serve as 'felts'. Place them on top of each other on one board, the smallest at the bottom and the largest on top. Moisten the mound with water and cover with another cloth.

Making a sheet of paper

It is essential to work quickly when drawing the first sheet of paper. However, if you are not happy with the result, just immerse the mould and deckle in the vat and start again.

1 Place the deckle over the mesh side of the mould.

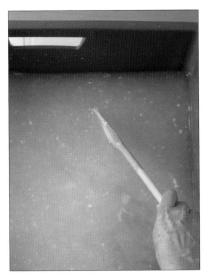

2 Agitate the pulp with your hand or a wooden spoon.

4 Pull up the mould and deckle and allow to drain, keeping it level. Shake from side to side and up and down to settle the fibres.

6 Extra decorative materials, such as flower petals, can be sprinkled on the newly drawn sheet if desired.

3 Quickly and confidently dip the mould and deckle into the vat, using a scooping movement. Keep the mould and deckle level under the surface.

5 Remove the deckle. A sheet of pulp should be evenly deposited on the mesh.

Couching a sheet of paper

When couching, you can decide either to make a single sheet, or produce a whole sequence of sheets at the same size. When piling them on top of one another, insert cloths in between each sheet.

2 With one continuous smooth movement, press the mould and pulp down firmly on to the mound.

4 Place another damp cloth on top of the sheet of pulp, making sure there are no wrinkles. Continue in this way until you have up to six sheets, known as a 'post'. Add more pulp to the vat as you continue, otherwise the sheets will become too thin.

1 Work quickly when couching. Place the long left-hand edge of the mould on to the long right-hand side of the couching mound at a 90° angle.

3 Lift the opposite edge of the mould, depositing the sheet of pulp on to the dish towel or 'felt'.

Pressing

This is only necessary if you require a smooth surface to the paper. Beautiful sheets can be created without pressing, where the natural texture of the paper, and of any added materials, can be seen.

1 Each post of papers needs to be pressed to remove some of the water. Place folded newspapers on top of the final felt and then place the second pressing board on top of the newspapers.

2 Turn the 'sandwich' over. Remove the base board and couching mound and replace with more folded newspapers then place the base board back in position. Stand on the boards or use heavy weights to expel the water.

Drying

The paper sheets will dry surprisingly quickly, often within a few hours, although more time should be allowed for thicker sheets.

1 Carefully remove the top board and newspapers. The sheets can be carefully peeled away from the felts and allowed to dry naturally.

2 Alternatively, place the sheets on a flat Perspex (Plexiglas ®) board and leave to dry, first sponging them to remove excess water. This will give a smoother quality. It is also possible to smooth them carefully with an iron.

Sizing

Sizing paper is not an essential requirement, but it will protect the paper and is important if you are intending to write on the surface.

1 Dissolve 5ml/1 tsp of gelatine or agar-agar with about 1 litre (2 pints) of hot water in a shallow bowl. Working quickly before the mixture hardens, dip each sheet of paper in the bowl, then lay it on a cloth. Put the sized papers on a Perspex board.

2 Alternatively brush each sheet with PVA (white) glue diluted with water (15ml/1 tbsp of glue to 750ml/1¼ pints water) then lay on a kitchen cloth on a Perspex board.

3 You can also add household starch or PVA glue to the vat before forming sheets. Use 15–30ml/1–2 tbsp starch or glue to 4 litres (7 pints) water.

STRAW PAPER

Interesting paper can be made from almost any of the plants found in the garden or countryside, such as hay, straw, grass, irises, montbretia, gladioli, pampas grass, yucca, daffodils and foxgloves. Record each plant you use in a notebook, with a small sample of the paper attached. Make a note of which part of the plant was used, the time of year it was gathered and how long the fibres were beaten. Straw can be gleaned from the fields after harvesting and is also available from pet shops. Be careful not to collect rare or protected wild plants.

1 Select your plant materials. If using plants other than straw, firstly remove any tough woody stalks and plant debris.

2 Cut the straw or other plant material into lengths of about 2½cm (1in). About 115g (4oz) of straw was used here.

3 Half-fill a pan with straw, then add water so it is two-thirds full. Leave overnight. Wearing rubber gloves, add 60–75ml/4–5 tbsp of washing soda crystals and bring to the boil, stirring occasionally. Simmer for 1–2 hours until soft. Test the plant matter by rubbing it between your gloved fingers – if it feels soft and separates easily, it is ready.

4 Leave the mixture to cool or add cold water. Place the net curtain fabric in a sieve supported over a bowl and pour the straw mixture through. Rinse with running water until the water runs clear. The most effective way of doing this is by knotting the two opposite corners of the net fabric together then hang the loop over a tap.

SAFETY NOTE
Tough, woody plants may need to be boiled in a solution of caustic soda (lye or sodium hydroxide) instead of washing soda crystals (sodium carbonate). Use caustic soda with great caution. Wear rubber gloves and plastic goggles, and always add the caustic soda to a generous amount of water. Never add the water to the caustic soda or it will cause a chemical reaction and may splash into your face.

▶

Materials and Equipment You Will Need
Straw or other plant material • Large scissors • Large stainless steel or enamel pan • Rubber gloves • Safety goggles • Tablespoon • Washing soda crystals (sodium carbonate) • Square of net curtain fabric • Sieve (strainer) • Plastic bowl or bucket • Plastic or glass measuring jug (cup) • Liquidizer or heavy-duty plastic and flat piece of wood or mallet • Glass jar • Large rectangular plastic bowl • Mould and deckle • Pressing boards • Couching cloths • Palette knife (optional)

5 Put a small amount of straw fibres in a liquidizer, fill with water and liquidize in short bursts. Alternatively, you can beat the fibres by hand. Wrap a small amount in heavy-duty plastic and beat it with a flat piece of wood, opening the plastic occasionally to add water. Save some of the unbeaten straw to add texture to the paper.

6 Test the fibres by placing a pinch in a glass jar. Cover with your hand or the lid and shake vigorously. The separated fibres should float freely. If there are still clumps of fibre stuck together, you need to continue the beating process.

7 Pour enough clean water into the large, deep plastic bowl to accommodate your mould and deckle easily. Add the straw pulp. You will need less pulp than for recycled paper as the fibres are longer.

8 Make a sheet of paper (see Basic Techniques). As you lift the mould and deckle out of the vat, rock it from side to side as the water drains off to spread the fibres evenly over the surface.

9 Couch the sheet (see Basic Techniques). Alternatively, leave it to air dry naturally for a few hours on the mould, in which case it will have one textured side and one smooth side.

10 When the couched sheet is completely dry, press and dry it (see Basic Techniques). If air-dried on the mould, remove by rubbing the back of the mesh with your fingertips. Use a palette knife if necessary to lift the edge.

DYED PLANT PAPER

Dyeing plant fibres produces interesting effects as the dye mixes with the plant's natural colour. Bleaching the fibres first will result in brighter colours that are closer to the original dye colour. Experiment by using differently dyed fibres together to produce paper that looks one colour, but in close-up contains different-coloured fibres. The paper here is made from yucca leaves which have been boiled for about 4 hours with soda ash (anhydrous sodium carbonate). They make an attractive coloured paper that is strong and textured.

1 Weigh the dry plant fibres and calculate the amount of warm water that is needed to allow them to move around freely in the dye bowl (about 1.5 litres/2½ pints) water to 115g/4oz dry fibres). Place the fibres in the bowl and add 500ml (17fl oz) of the total amount of water.

2 To prepare the dye bath, and wearing rubber gloves, an apron and a face mask, dissolve 15ml/1 tbsp of dye powder in a small amount of warm water. Stir thoroughly and check that no grains of powder remain. Pour half of the remaining water into the second bowl. Add the dissolved dye and stir well.

3 Weigh 10g (¼oz) washing soda crystals and dissolve in the remaining water. Then weigh out 60g (2½oz) salt.

►

Materials and Equipment You Will Need
Plastic sheet, to cover work surface • Measuring scales • Plant fibres • Plastic or glass measuring jug (cup) • 2 plastic or glass bowls • Rubber gloves • Plastic apron • Face mask (respirator) • Tablespoon • Dye powder • Washing soda (sodium carbonate) crystals • Wooden spoon • Salt • Piece of net curtain fabric • Colander • Large rectangular plastic bowl • Mould and deckle • 2 pressing boards • Couching cloths

4 Add the plant fibres to the dye bath and stir for 5 minutes. Add half the salt and stir well for another 5 minutes. Leave to stand for 5 minutes, then add the remaining salt and stir for 5 minutes. Stir regularly for an additional 15 minutes. Add half the dissolved washing soda crystals over about 5 minutes, stirring well. Stir continuously for 15 minutes. Add the remaining soda and stir well. Continue to stir regularly for 30 minutes for pale shades, or 45 minutes for deep shades.

6 Use the fibre pulp to form sheets of paper (see Basic Techniques). Press the sheets for a smoother finish, or air-dry them to emphasize the natural textures.

5 Carefully drain the dyed plant fibres through a piece of net curtain fabric placed inside a colander. Rinse under running water until the water runs clear.

DYEING INSTRUCTIONS
Protect your work area with a sheet of plastic. At all times during the dyeing, wear rubber gloves and a plastic apron. Also wear a face mask (respirator) when mixing the dye powder as it is very fine and should not be inhaled. Use only plastic or glass equipment as these materials can easily be washed and will not affect the dye. Keep your dyeing equipment separate and don't use it for other purposes. The quantity of dye quoted is for a mid-shade; increase or decrease the amount to alter the depth of colour. Use warm, not hot, water at all stages.

GREETINGS CARD

Several interesting handmade papers are used to make this card. The orange paper has scraps of fabric and thread incorporated in the pulp, as well as natural dye from boiled onion skins. The contrast papers are decorated with vetch and clover leaves, which were sprinkled on the wet sheets before couching. Extra texture and detail is added with a silk embroidery thread (floss), stitching through the paper as you would stitch fabric. The ingeniously folded envelope creates a perfect finishing touch.

1 Neatly tear a 19 x 14cm (7½ x 5½in) rectangle from the thick paper. Fold in half to make a card shape.

3 Tear small squares, strips and triangles from the other papers. Arrange and glue in place on the card to make an attractive design. Using silk thread, decorate the design with stitches.

5 Fold in the other two corners to form an envelope.

2 Tear a 7 x 6cm (2¾ x 2½in) rectangle from contrasting paper. Position it centrally on the front of the card and glue in place.

4 Sign the card and place diagonally in the centre of the A4 sheet. Then fold in the opposite corners.

6 Tie decorative ribbons neatly around the envelope to match the colours found in the papers.

Materials and Equipment You Will Need
Thick handmade paper • Assorted handmade papers, in contrasting colours (see Basic Techniques) • Paper glue •
Silk embroidery thread (floss) • Sewing needle • Scissors • A4 (8½ x 11in) sheet of handmade paper, for the envelope • Ribbon

EMBEDDED LEAVES

In this elegant triptych, leaves or grasses are trapped between two layers of pulp. You can also embed plants with flowers in the same way. Aluminium mesh, available from car accessory stores or hardware stores for repairing holes in bodywork, is used as a temporary mould. As a variation, you can make a partial lift of pulp from the vat; this gives a softer, textured effect and leaves more of the plants exposed. Another possibility is to cut geometric shapes out of mesh and embed them in the pulp as a contrast to the plant material. The finished triptych looks best displayed in a double Perspex (Plexiglas ®) free-standing frame so that you can appreciate its translucency.

1 Gather leaves and grasses with interesting-shaped leaves or textured stems, and attractive colours.

2 Using scissors, cut a strip of aluminium mesh 4.5 x 25cm (1¾ x 10in), taking care to avoid the sharp, serrated edges. Place the pulp in the bowl (see Basic Techniques).

3 Holding the mesh by the edges as shown, lift a strip of pulp out of the bowl.

▶

Materials and Equipment You Will Need
Selection of leaves and grasses • Strong scissors • Aluminium mesh • Finely beaten white recycled paper pulp •
Large rectangular plastic bowl • Couching cloths • 2 pressing boards

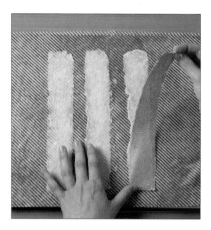

4 Couch the pulp on the cloths (see Basic Techniques). Repeat to make three narrow sheets altogether, couching them side by side with 1–1.5cm (½–⅝in) gap between them.

6 Lift three more strips of pulp in the same way. Place these on top of the first strips, covering the plant material. Place a pressing board on top and press (see Basic Techniques).

7 Having arranged the plant material on a wet sheet, an alternative is to lift a partial strip of pulp. Dip the edge of the mesh furthest from you back in the vat and move the mesh towards you, lifting it out at the same time. This will wash off some of the pulp. Couch this over the top of the strips. Leave to dry naturally.

5 Arrange the plant material on the wet pulp, extending it over the edge of the paper or on to the next strip of pulp.

8 Another suggestion is to cut geometric shapes out of aluminium mesh and use them to couch pulp on top of the plant material, leaving gaps. Press the sheets well to incorporate the mesh.

LEAF COLLAGE

This beautiful design originates with small sheets of white paper cast over leaf shapes, using a small mould and deckle made from two picture frames. The leaf shapes used here are fabric relief forms, but actual leaves are just as effective. The leaf-embossed sheets are arranged on a backing sheet sprinkled with rose petals and the design is painted with watercolours in pink, grey and purple. Frayed strips of fabric, dyed leaves and scraps of other handmade papers add to the effect. Choose your own fragments to make your design truly original.

1 Tear the white paper into postage-stamp-sized pieces. Soak for 2 hours in a bucket of water, then liquidize into pulp (see Basic Techniques).

2 Place the pulp in a glass or plastic bowl that will accommodate the small mould and deckle easily.

3 Place six leaf shapes on to cloths on top of a pressing board. Using the small deckle and mould, couch a sheet of pulp over each shape (see Basic Techniques).

Materials and Equipment You Will Need
Pieces of white paper • Plastic bucket • Liquidizer • Glass or plastic bowl • Leaf shapes • Couching cloths • Pressing board • Small mould and deckle •
A4 (8½ x 11in) size mould and deckle • Flower petals • Selection of handmade Indian papers and fabric remnants • Incense stick •
PVA (white) glue • Brush, for applying glue • Watercolour paints, in pink, grey and purple • Artist's paintbrush • Dyed honesty leaves

4 Make six small sheets and leave them to dry naturally.

5 Make an A4 sheet of paper, using the larger mould and deckle. You may then need to use a larger bowl for the pulp.

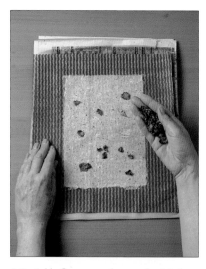

6 Sprinkle flower petals over the A4 sheet while the pulp is still wet. Leave to dry.

7 From your collection of handmade papers and fabric remnants, tear two long strips 38 x 5cm (15 x 2in) and 38 x 6cm (15 x 2½in). Fray the edges of the fabric and burn the edges of the paper strip with an incense stick.

8 When dry, seal all the pieces of paper with diluted PVA glue (1 part water to 1 part glue). Leave to dry, then paint with watercolour paints.

9 Group the leaf papers into a formal arrangement and glue to the A4 base paper. Attach dyed honesty leaves to the centre panel with dots of PVA glue.

EMBOSSED WRITING PAPER

Embossing is a very effective way of decorating handmade paper. A simple motif or initials cut into thick card or a design made out of coiled string is pressed into the surface of the paper. The notepaper and envelope in this project are both embossed. Size, in the form of gelatine, is added to the paper pulp so that ink will not seep into the paper fibres. Drying the sheets on a smooth surface such as a kitchen counter will give a suitable flat surface for writing. You can also iron the sheets when dry, but take care not to flatten the embossing.

1 Make a mould and deckle for the writing paper, with inner measurements 21 x 15cm (8½ x 6in) (see Basic Techniques). The envelope mould is 21 x 29cm (8½ x 11⅞in). For the deckle cut a piece of fibreboard the same size as the mould, open out an envelope, place in the centre and draw round it. Cut the shape out very carefully, using a craft knife and cutting mat. Varnish the deckle.

2 Draw a simple shape on cardboard and cut out with the craft knife.

3 Prepare the vat (see Basic Techniques). Dissolve the gelatine in 50ml (2fl oz) cup of warm water and stir it into the water in the vat. Mix in the paper pulp. Using the writing paper mould and deckle, make a fairly thick sheet of paper and couch it on to cloths on a pressing board (see Basic Techniques).

4 Place your chosen embossing shape on the sheet of paper, positioning it as desired.

5 Cover the sheet with several layers of cloths. Place the second pressing board on top and press (see Basic Techniques).

6 Remove the top cloths. Carefully turn over the embossed sheet of paper, still on the base cloth, and place on a smooth surface to dry. Repeat steps 4–6 as many times as required.

▶

Materials and Equipment You Will Need

Mould and deckle, for the paper • Mould and fibreboard deckle, for the envelope • Envelope • Craft (utility) knife • Cutting mat • Acrylic varnish • Decorator's brush, for applying varnish • Pencil • Cardboard • Large rectangular plastic bowl • ½ packet of gelatine • White recycled paper pulp • Couching cloths • 2 pressing boards • Metal ruler • Bone folder or straight edge • Paper glue • Scissors • Double-sided adhesive tape

7 Using the envelope mould and fibreboard deckle, make a sheet of paper. Carefully wipe away any pulp on the edges of the deckle.

8 After draining, carefully lift off the deckle, couch the sheet and position the embossing shape. Make as many envelope sheets as required. Leave to dry.

9 Crease and fold the envelope sheets, using a ruler and the flat side of a bone folder or straight edge. Score along the line of the fold using the flat side of the bone folder. Lay the ruler along the line of the fold and holding the ruler firmly, crease upwards. Repeat on all four sides of the envelope. Crease firmly using the flat side of the bone folder through a protective paper, so that the envelope does not become shiny.

10 Turn in the side flaps, then glue the deep flap to the side flaps.

11 Cut a piece of double-sided tape to fit the remaining flap and place along the edge. Peel off the protective strip to seal the envelope.

PATTERNED PULP

This stunning sheet of paper is built up in several layers, using four different colours of recycled paper pulp. The chequerboard squares and stripes and the large spiral motif are all created with simple handmade stencils. The different-coloured layers of pulp fuse with the background sheet during the pressing process. Experiment with your own stencil shapes and your own choice of colours to make an individual sheet of paper that is decorative enough to frame and hang on the wall.

1 Liquidize the white paper into pulp (see Basic Techniques). Make four different-coloured pulps by adding a teaspoon of each colour powder to a small quantity of pulp.

2 Using the red pulp, make a sheet of paper and couch it on to the cloths (see Basic Techniques).

3 Cut a strip of card the same length as the longest edge of the red sheet. Bend it into four equal sections to form a square stencil, then tape the ends together. Place the stencil on the mould.

►

Materials and Equipment You Will Need
Liquidizer • Pieces of white paper • Teaspoon • Water-based powder colours, in yellow, red, blue and purple • Large rectangular plastic bowl • Mould and deckle • Couching cloths • 2 pressing boards • Scissors • Thin card (stock) • Adhesive tape • 4 plastic cups • Pencil • Craft (utility) knife • Cutting mat

4 Using a plastic cup, pour some yellow pulp into the stencil. Remove the stencil and couch the yellow square on top of the red sheet, starting in one corner. Make six yellow squares, couching them on the red sheet in a chequered pattern.

6 Remove the stencil and couch a blue stripe on to the chequered sheet, positioning it as shown. Repeat to make four blue stripes altogether.

8 Place the spiral stencil on the mould and pour in some purple pulp. Remove the stencil and couch the purple spiral on to the centre of the patterned sheet. Press the sheet using the second pressing board until dry (see Basic Techniques).

5 Cut a second strip of card and bend this to make a rectangular stencil. Place the rectangle on the mould and pour in some blue pulp.

7 Cut a piece of card the same size as the wet sheet. Draw a spiral shape using the template at the back of the book. Using a craft knife and cutting mat, cut out and remove the shape. The remaining card forms a stencil.

TEXTURED SURFACE

One of the most exciting things about making your own paper is that you can manipulate it when it is wet. After pressing, a sheet of paper can be pushed and pulled around to a surprising degree. For this design, decide which your base colour will be and make this sheet twice as thick as usual, either by using very thick pulp or by couching two normal sheets on top of each other. The textured effect is created very simply with a plastic spray container. A mould is used without the deckle to support the paper while you are working on it.

1 Place the thick base paper sheet on the cloth. Carefully place the other two sheets on top. Place a second piece of cloth over these and lightly iron.

2 Cut a piece of net curtain at least 10cm (4in) larger all round than the mould. Place the mould in the tray, then place the net curtain on top. Remove the pressed paper from the cloth and place on the net, centred over the mould.

3 Set the spray container to produce a jet of water rather than a mist. Starting in the centre, squirt water on to the paper so that it makes a hole, pushing away the top two layers to reveal the colours of the base papers.

4 Make more holes all over the paper, stopping at regular intervals to let the water drain away. Be careful not to use the spray too vigorously or it may blow a hole right through the paper.

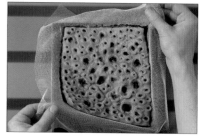

5 When the design is finished, allow the excess water to drain away. Carefully remove the paper from the mould by picking up the curtain. Leave the paper on the net curtain in a warm place to dry.

Materials and Equipment You Will Need
1 thick and 2 normal sheets of newly formed pressed paper, in different colours · Couching cloths · Iron · Scissors · Net curtain fabric · Mould · Shallow plastic tray, larger than your mould · Plastic spray container

LAMINATED PAPER

Tissue paper and glue, which dries clear, are built up in layers to make this paper. To add textural interest you can incorporate threads and wire, or leaves, pressed flowers and other flat objects. Use a thicker glue solution to laminate heavier objects. The finished paper has a light, translucent quality and is particularly suitable for displaying in front of a window or artificial light.

1 Prepare piles of yellow and turquoise tissue paper squares, about 10 x 10cm (4 x 4in). Tear circles out of the yellow squares and set aside. Tear another set of squares, about 8 x 8cm (3¼ x 3¼in).

2 Cut squares of scrim, about 8 x 8cm (3¼ x 3¼in). Clamp the brass wire into a small pair of pliers and twist it round the outer edge to form flat spiral shapes.

3 Dilute 2 parts PVA glue with 1 part water and brush over a sheet of green tissue paper on a plastic sheet. Place a large yellow square on the background sheet in the top left-hand corner. Put a turquoise square next to the yellow one, overlapping and brushing them with glue. Alternate the colours and the squares with circular holes on top, to create a chequerboard pattern.

4 Glue the smaller tissue squares on top of the squares without holes, placing them diagonally. Glue the scrim squares diagonally over the squares with holes.

5 Glue the yellow circles on to the turquoise squares.

6 Place the brass wire spirals on the scrim squares and cover with a generous coat of thicker glue. Leave the finished laminated sheet on a flat surface to dry overnight. When it is completely dry, peel off the plastic backing.

Materials and Equipment You Will Need
Tissue paper, in green, yellow and turquoise • Scissors • Scrim • Thin brass wire • Small pair of pliers • PVA (white) glue • Container, for diluting glue • Brush, for applying glue • Large sheet of pale yellow tissue paper, about 50 x 38cm (20 x 15in) • Plastic sheet

ROSE PETAL RELIEF

This project focuses on finding interesting shapes to use as moulds for cast paper pulp. The plastic form used here is from a DIY or hardware store and has a regular relief pattern deep enough to contain decorative materials such as rose petals. There are many such plastic forms, such as detachable plastic shelf supports or rawl-plugs and each one gives the design an original style. Framing this in a matching paper frame adds an extra dimension. The chosen shape needs to fit inside a plastic light switch plate, from which the frame is cast.

1 Make the paper into pulp (see Basic Techniques). Drain it through a sieve to remove water and make the pulp thicker.

2 Place the plastic form and the light switch plate face down on a couching cloth laid on a flat surface. Spoon pulp over the edges of the light switch plate to make a square frame. Spoon more pulp over the whole of the plastic form.

3 Press the pulp flat with a small sponge to compress it and remove water. Leave to dry naturally.

Materials and Equipment You Will Need
Pieces of cream or white paper • Liquidizer • Plastic measuring jug (cup) • Sieve (strainer) • Small plastic relief form • Plastic light switch plate • Couching cloths • Dessert spoon • Small sponge • PVA (white) glue container • Brush, for applying glue • Varnished wooden frame • Watercolour paints • Artist's paintbrush • Dried rose petals or other decorative materials

▶

4 Remove the two paper shapes from the forms. Seal with diluted PVA glue (1 part water to 1 part glue).

6 Seal the paper form again with dilute PVA glue, then paint with watercolours. Use colours to complement the rose petals, using delicately blended watercolour paints. Paint the paper frame made from the finger plate in a similar colour scheme.

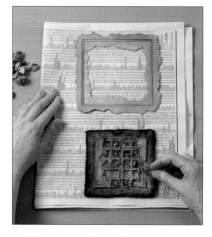

7 Glue rose petals or other materials into the recesses of the paper form, using dots of PVA glue.

5 Place the cast paper form face down on a couching cloth, then place a small wooden frame over it. Using thicker pulp, spoon it over the edges of the paper form to make a square shape that is contained by the frame. Leave to dry naturally, then carefully remove the paper form and the wooden frame.

8 Carefully glue the paper frame on to the paper form.

PAPER BOWLS

These little bowls are a delightful way to present small gifts, or to hold chocolates on a dinner table. They are very simple to make and allow for any number of variations at each stage. You could omit the ribbon and use just one sheet of paper, or the ribbon could be replaced by feathers. After pressing the circles together, you could remove small pieces from the top layer of paper to reveal the paper and ribbon underneath. The paper is used at the stage where it is newly formed and can readily be moulded into shape.

1 Cut a paper circle large enough to cover three-quarters of the orange. Cut a circle in card to this size, and a second circle smaller than the first. Cut eight equal lengths of curling ribbon.

2 Place the green paper on a couching cloth, with the large card circle on top. Holding it down firmly, tear away the green paper up to the edge of the card.

3 Place the strips of curling ribbon across the paper circle so that they look like the spokes of a wheel.

4 Using the small card circle, tear out a red paper circle in the same way.

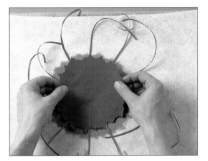

5 Lift up the red circle and place it on top of the green circle. Place a couching cloth on top then press the circles together, using a rolling pin. The cloth will absorb some moisture from the damp paper.

6 Remove the wet cloth. Carefully pick up both paper circles together and, turning them over, place them on a dry piece of couching cloth. ▶

Materials and Equipment You Will Need

Paper • Orange • Scissors • Thin card (stock) • Narrow curling ribbon • Sheets of newly formed and lightly pressed paper in green and red • 4 large couching cloths • Rolling pin

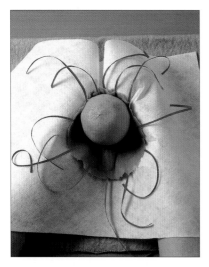

7 Place an orange in the centre of the circles. Using the cloth for support, draw up the paper circles and form them around the orange.

9 Remove the cloth and leave the paper bowl in a warm place until it is completely dry. Ease the bowl away from the orange by opening up the paper a little without it tearing or losing its shape. Finally, curl the ribbons.

8 Bunch the cloth very tightly at the top. Squeeze to remove more moisture and press the paper around the orange.

NOTEPAPER CASE

This sea-blue folder is made from a sheet of paper very simply embossed with the distinctive shape of a shell. The paper is lined and coated with glue to give it extra strength. In a project such as this it is important to fold the paper well, using either a traditional bone folder or the back of a scissor blade. The dimensions quoted here will fit notepaper 10.5 x 15cm (4¼ x 6in) and envelopes 11 x 16cm (4½ x 6¼in). If you are making it as a gift, you could design notepaper embossed with the same motif and in different shades of blue.

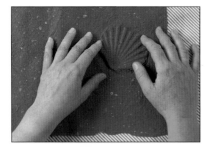

1 Wipe the shell with a little petroleum jelly and place in position on a cloth. Make a sheet of paper at least 35 x 30cm (14 x 12in), using blue pulp and couch it on to the cloth, covering the shell (see Basic Techniques).

2 Leave to dry, then remove the shell. Dilute 1 part PVA glue with 5 parts water and brush over the paper.

3 When the paper is dry, line the embossed sheet with thin plant paper, brushing it sparingly with glue. When completely dry, cut out a rectangle 32 x 26cm (12½ x 10¼in). Following the template at the back of the book, mark the fold lines and cut the corners using a craft knife and cutting mat.

4 Score along all the fold lines, using a bone folder or the back of a scissor blade and a ruler. Fold the paper inwards along the scored lines.

5 Cut slots for the ribbon as marked and thread it through.

Materials and Equipment You Will Need

Shell • Petroleum jelly • Couching cloth • Recycled paper pulp, dyed blue • Large rectangular plastic bowl • Mould and deckle • PVA (white) glue • Container, for diluting glue • Brush, for applying glue • Thin plant paper • Scissors • Craft (utility) knife • Cutting mat • Bone folder or straight edge (optional) • Ruler • Purple ribbon

FINGER PLATE

Finger plates (push plates) were designed as practical items to protect doors from finger marks. They can also be used as an effective decorative focus on a door. This plain Perspex (Plexiglas ®) finger plate has been transformed by decorating it with a repeat design of three-dimensional paper motifs. In this project thick paper pulp is used to take casts of the shape, which can be any raised motif of suitable size.

2 Spoon the thick pulp on to your raised shape to make a cast, squeezing the pulp to remove water. Make three casts and leave to dry naturally.

1 Make the scrap paper into pulp (see Basic Techniques). Drain it through a sieve to remove excess water and make a thicker pulp.

3 Place a cloth on a flat surface and carefully draw round the Perspex finger plate, using a pencil.

4 Place the paper shapes face down in the centre of the plate outline.

▶

Materials and Equipment You Will Need

Cream or white scrap paper • Liquidizer • Sieve (strainer) • Plastic measuring jug (cup) • Glass or plastic bowl • Dessert spoon • Decorative raised shape • Couching cloth • Pencil • Perspex (Plexiglas ®) finger plate (push plate) • 4 pieces of wood • Scissors • PVA (white) glue • Container, for glue • Soft paintbrush, for glue • Watercolour paints or coloured inks • Artist's paintbrush • Brass screws

5 Cut four lengths of wood to form a frame slightly larger than the plate outline to allow for shrinkage.

7 Remove the pieces of wood to reveal the dry paper.

9 Cut the paper along the drawn outline. Dampen the ends of the paper and press on to the screw holes of the finger plate for a perfect fit.

6 Spoon pulp into the wooden mould, covering the cast shapes and the pencil outline. Leave to dry.

8 Place the Perspex finger plate over the dry paper and draw round it.

10 Using a soft paintbrush, seal the paper with diluted PVA glue (1 part water to 1 part glue) then decorate with watercolours or inks. Place the paper under the Perspex plate and attach securely to the door with brass screws.

STATIONERY FOLDER

This colourful folder is simply decorated with bright red spots, using different-sized rings cut from a plastic cup as stencils. The fastening ties are trapped between two sheets of pulp, so it is sturdy and practical. The A3 sheet folds in half to make an ideal folder for A4 documents. If your mould and deckle is not this large, several smaller overlapping sheets will be equally strong.

1 Using dark blue pulp, make an A3 (11 x 17in) sheet of paper and couch on to cloths on a pressing board (see Basic Techniques).

2 Cut three lengths of cord, to make ties. Lay them on the wet sheet, one in the centre of each short side and two equally spaced on each long side.

4 Cut a plastic cup into rings to make simple stencils.

3 Cover with a second layer of dark blue pulp. Press lightly with a cloth to remove any air bubbles.

Materials and Equipment You Will Need

Recycled paper pulps, coloured dark blue and red • Mould and deckle • Large rectangular plastic bowl • Couching cloths • 2 pressing boards • Scissors • Thin cord • Plastic cups • Metal ruler • Blunt knife

5 Place the stencils randomly on a mould and pour in some red pulp.

6 Couch the red circles on to the dark blue sheet. Repeat until the sheet is covered with circles. Press and dry the decorated sheet (see Basic Techniques).

7 Using a metal ruler and a blunt knife, lightly score across the centre of the dry sheet to make the fold line.

8 Fold the sheet of decorated paper in half and fasten with the ties to close the stationery folder.

HAMMERED FRAME

This antique-looking frame is created with a plastic light switch surround which is used as a mould. The mottled cream pulp is made from two shades of scrap paper, and is deliberately applied to create an irregular shape. Texture is added by embedding beads in the wet pulp, and by indentations made by a small hammer. You can experiment with various textural effects by embedding other small objects in the pulp, such as buttons, threads or wire. The final frame is stained with tea or brown paint to give it an aged appearance.

1 Mixing both shades of paper, make the scrap paper into pulp (see Basic Techniques). Drain it through a sieve.

3 Spoon pulp over the beads and the light switch plate, allowing it to spread over the edges of the plate.

5 Press a small hammer randomly into the wet pulp to make a textured border. Leave to dry naturally, then remove the mould. Seal with diluted PVA glue (1 part glue to 1 part water).

2 Lay a couching cloth on a flat surface then place the light switch plate face down on top. Arrange the beads randomly on the plastic surface.

4 Sponge the pulp gently to remove any excess water.

6 For an antique effect, stain the frame with tea or brown watercolour paint.

Materials and Equipment You Will Need
White and cream paper scraps • Liquidizer • Sieve (strainer) • Couching cloth • Plastic light switch plate • Cream or pearl beads • Dessert spoon • Small sponge • Small hammer • PVA (white) glue • Container, for diluting glue • Brush, for applying glue • Tea or brown watercolour paint • Artist's paintbrush

LAMINATED CIRCLES

This laminated paper incorporates several techniques, including wax resist and ink. Instead of candle wax, you could use masking fluid or masking tape as a resist. Handle the thin tissue paper carefully, especially when it is wet. Once laminated with glue, the finished paper is quite strong and would be suitable for covering a book or as a special gift wrap. The strands of red embroidery threads (floss) are added at the end to create accents of colour in contrast to the blurred, painterly effect of the inked circles.

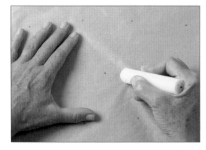

1 Using a pencil, mark small dots on the pale yellow tissue paper 8cm (3¼in) apart. Circle round each mark with the round end of the candle, pressing quite hard.

3 Tear circles of turquoise tissue paper, about 4cm (1½in) diameter. Cut lengths of red embroidery thread, about 6cm (2½in) long.

5 Place the embroidery threads on the turquoise circles, to make informal crosses. Cover with a generous coat of glue.

2 Place a plastic sheet under the tissue paper. Using a paintbrush and with the marks as a guide, brush the ink inside and slightly overlapping the wax circles. Leave on a flat surface out of direct sunlight.

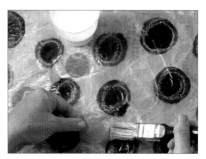

4 Dilute 2 parts PVA glue with 1 part water and brush all over the dry sheet of tissue paper. Place the turquoise circles in the gaps between the inked circles and brush over with some more glue.

6 Leave the finished paper on a flat surface to dry overnight. When it is completely dry, peel off the plastic backing.

Materials and Equipment You Will Need
Pencil • Sheet of pale yellow tissue paper, about 50 x 38cm (20 x 15in) • Plain white candle, diameter about 4cm (1½in) • Large sheet of plastic • Large artist's paintbrush • Blue or black ink • Turquoise tissue paper • Scissors • Red embroidery thread (floss) • PVA (white) glue • Container, for diluting glue • Brush, for applying glue

EMBROIDERED TRIANGLES

This richly textured sheet of paper is made using a mould on its own without the deckle to give an attractive uneven edge. It is then painted a bright background colour and decorated with various embroidery threads (flosses), gauze triangles and tiny beads, by stitching through the paper as you would fabric. Vilene attached to the back of the paper prevents it from tearing during the stitching. Create your own work of art by using a different colour for the painted background or by drawing your own design.

1 Make a sheet of paper, about 16 x 22cm (6¼ x 8½in), using a mould without the deckle (see Basic Techniques). Leave to dry thoroughly then peel off the mould, using a knife to lift the edge.

2 Paint one side of the paper with turquoise acrylic paint diluted with water. Leave to dry then iron between two sheets of tissue paper.

3 Using a ruler and pencil, draw a rectangle 10 x 16cm (4 x 6¼in) on the painted paper. Divide this into a grid of 2cm (¾in) squares.

▶

Materials and Equipment You Will Need
White paper pulp • Mould • Large Plastic bowl • Knife • Turquoise acrylic paint • Large paintbrush • Container for diluting paint • Iron • 2 sheets of tissue paper • Ruler • Pencil • Pastel coloured pencils (dark blue, green, orange and cerise) • Scissors • Vilene or backing cloth for stitching • Dressmaker's pins • Embroidery needles • Thick threads (floss) for couching, in dark blue and metallic gold • Matt and shiny embroidery threads, in dark blue, metallic gold, green, orange and cerise • Organza, in blue and red • Small beads • Thin plastic gloves • Antique gold finish • Mount (mat) board, cut to size • Strong dark blue thread

4 Using pastel pencils, colour the squares to form a multicoloured triangular grid.

6 Cut small triangles of blue and red organza. Stitch in place, adding a small bead in the centre.

8 Stitch the finished piece to the mount board using a strong dark blue thread.

5 Cut a piece of backing cloth larger than the design and pin to the back of the paper. Couch the thick dark blue thread along the lines outlining the rectangle (see Diagram 1). Couch all the grid lines in metallic gold, stitching along the horizontal lines first, then the vertical lines. Remove the pins and stitch the rest of the design in straight stitch, matching the thread colours to the pastel colours.

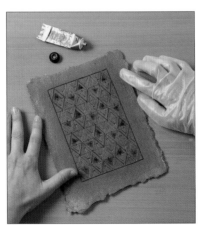

7 Wearing plastic gloves, rub the edges of the paper outside the design with antique gold paint.

COUCHING

Lay a thick thread along one of the drawn lines. Hold it in place at regular intervals with small stitches through the paper and backing cloth (see Diagram 1). Use sewing thread for the straight stitching, matching the colour to the couching thread or alternatively using a contrasting colour thread.

DIAGRAM 1

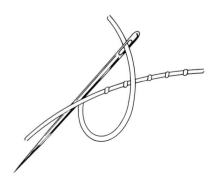

JAPANESE-BOUND BOOK

This attractive little book uses the traditional Japanese four-hole binding technique to enclose various soft plant papers for the 'leaves', or pages. The textured paper for the front and back covers was made by incorporating chopped-up plant materials and fresh herbs in the paper pulp before forming the sheets. Instead of raffia you could use linen, string or a strong embroidery thread (floss) for the binding.

1 Fold the two sheets of plant paper in half, as shown, for the front and back covers. Individually fold the other sheets in the same way.

2 Place all the sheets with the folded edges together, and the front and back covers in position. Hold the folded edges in place with two bulldog clips.

3 Place the sheets on a cutting mat. Using a ruler, trim the edge opposite the folds with a craft knife. This will be the spine.

4 Mark four equidistant points 1.5cm (⅝in) in from the spine, starting 1.5cm (⅝in) from the top and bottom of the book. Using a bradawl or awl, make a hole at each marked point through all thicknesses of the paper.

5 Thread a length of raffia in the needle. Insert it between the 'leaves' of the spine, leaving about 6cm (2½in) for tying later. Bring the needle up through the second hole from the bottom, then take it round the spine and back through the same hole, pulling gently.

Materials and Equipment You Will Need

2 A4 (8½ x 11in) sheets of handmade plant paper • 8 A4 (8½ x 11in) sheets of assorted handmade papers • 2 bulldog clips • Cutting mat • Metal ruler • Craft (utility) knife • Pencil • Bradawl or awl • Large-eyed needle • Natural raffia

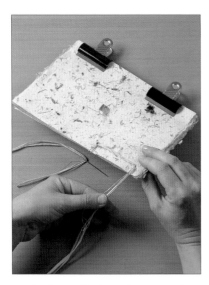

6 Take the needle down the spine to the bottom hole and repeat.

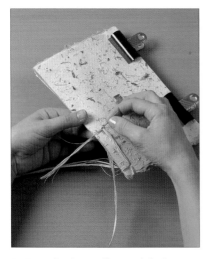

7 Now take the needle round the lower edge of the book and back through the bottom hole, then back up the spine of the book on the opposite side and through the original hole.

8 Repeat with the remaining two holes until you are back at the starting point. Remove the bulldog clips.

9 Take the needle back between the 'leaves' to the original end of raffia. Tie the two ends securely, then tuck the knot into the spine.

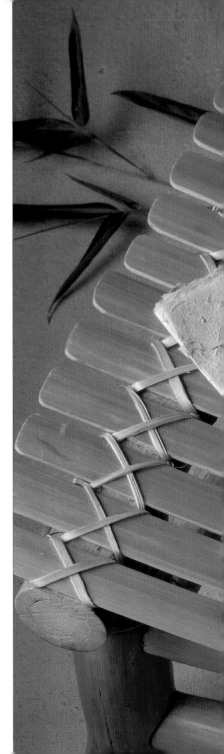

EASTERN MOBILE

The natural colours and textures of wooden sticks and white handmade paper blend harmoniously in this mobile that is reminiscent of the Orient. A stylized paper leaf shape is glued to the triangular frame, and this simple motif is repeated in the large leaves which hang below. If you place the mobile near an open window, the suspended leaves will move in the breeze.

1 Using white scrap paper, make a batch of pulp (see Basic Techniques). Add 10ml (2 tsp) PVA glue and stir in.

3 Cut reasonably even wooden sticks into gradually shorter lengths. Cut nine or ten lengths altogether.

5 Lay out the sticks to form a triangle. Thread the wire through the holes, wrapping the ends of the wire around the first and last sticks to secure them.

2 Couch plenty of white paper sheets on to couching cloths (see Basic Techniques).

4 Drill a small hole through the centre of each of the sticks.

6 Cover your work surface with a sheet of plastic. Tear up some of the white paper to make a simple leaf shape which will fit on to the triangle. Paint the paper lightly with diluted PVA glue and press on to the sticks. ▶

Materials and Equipment You Will Need

White scrap paper • Liquidizer • Large rectangular plastic bowl • Plastic teaspoon • PVA (white) glue • Mould and deckle • Couching cloths • Hacksaw • Wooden sticks • Hand drill • Soft wire • Large plastic sheet • Container, for diluting glue • Brush, for applying glue • Thin, pliable twigs • Sewing needle • White sewing cotton • Screw eye or hook

7 Wire thin twigs together to form five large leaf shapes.

9 Using a needle, thread long lengths of white cotton through the tip of each leaf.

10 Tie the leaves to the wooden sticks, using varying lengths of cotton thread.

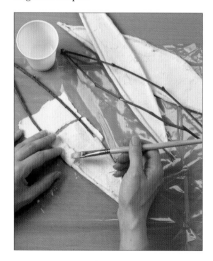

8 Tear up more white paper. Paint lightly with PVA glue and wrap around the twig leaf shapes. Leave all the shapes to dry.

11 Attach a screw eye or hook near the top of the mobile, in the centre, for hanging the mobile.

MIXED PULP NOTEBOOK

Use a special decorative or experimental sheet of your own handmade paper to make the cover of this notebook. The brightly coloured paper used here was created by pouring five different-coloured pulps separately on to the mould. The sheet was couched as normal, then hung up to dry to keep the raised texture. The 'leaves' of the notebook are made from a single large sheet of Ingres paper, folded several times. Stitch the 'leaves' and cover together with a strong thread.

1 Dilute 1 part PVA glue with 5 parts water. Brush the diluted glue all over the decorative handmade paper which will be the cover, to give it extra strength. Leave to dry.

2 Line the cover with the Indian plant paper, using a thin layer of PVA glue. Leave to dry completely.

3 Using a craft knife and cutting mat and a ruler, trim the cover to make a rectangle about 26 x 19cm (10¼ x 7½in).

Materials and Equipment You Will Need

PVA (white) glue • Container, for diluting glue • Brush, for applying glue • Decorative sheet of handmade paper, A4 size (8½ x 11 in) or larger and thin enough to fold • Sheet of thin Indian plant paper • Craft (utility) knife • Cutting mat • Ruler • Sheet of thin Ingres paper, 50 x 70cm (20 x 27½in) • Blunt kitchen knife • Pencil • Long, strong, thick needle • Scissors • Thick linen or polyester thread (floss), in a colour to match your cover • Large button or bead • Bradawl or awl • Thin cord or leather thong

4 Fold the sheet of Ingres paper in half, lining up the corners exactly. Slice carefully along the fold for two-thirds of its length, using a blunt knife. Fold the sheet in half and cut again. Repeat until it is slightly smaller than the cover.

5 Using a pencil, mark the centre on the folded edge of the Ingres paper and a point 2cm (¾in) from each end. Open out the 'leaves' and pierce a hole through each mark with a needle, through to the inside fold.

6 Place the 'leaves' inside the cover. Mark matching points inside the cover on the fold line and pierce holes in the same way as before.

7 Cut a length of thread three times the length of the notebook. Thread the needle and begin sewing from the inside, through the centre hole of the 'leaves' and the cover.

8 Take the needle back through one of the outside holes, then right across the inside to the far hole, back through the outside and return through the centre hole. Pull the two ends tight and knot over the central inside thread. Trim the thread ends.

9 Stitch a button or bead to the front cover, near the edge. Keep the stitches wide apart for extra strength. Make two corresponding holes on the back cover with a bradawl or awl. Cut a length of cord or leather to make a loop for the button or bead. Thread this by hand through the holes, then knot the ends on the inside of the cover.

WALL-HUNG MEMORY QUILT

This is a lovely way to display a personal collection of photographs, postcards, tickets, programmes and other memorabilia, by incorporating them into a paper wall-hanging. If you plan to include handwritten texts, use a photocopy, otherwise the ink will 'bleed' on contact with the wet pulp. Adapt the size and number of the squares to suit your own material. The patchwork squares are held together with lengths of paper string or embroidery thread (floss), and also built into the paper are loops for hanging the finished piece on the wall.

1 With your collection of materials in front of you, decide on a standard size for each patch and the number of patches that are required.

2 Make temporary moulds from aluminium mesh. Cut a square 2.5cm (1in) larger all round than the size of the objects, and a strip 13 x 4cm (5 x 1½in). Fold strips of masking tape 13cm (5in) long over each edge of the mesh to cover the sharp edges.

3 Dye two or three batches of pulp, slightly thicker than normal (see Basic Techniques). Place in separate bowls. Holding the mesh by the edges, lift a square of pulp out of the first bowl.

▶

Materials and Equipment You Will Need
Collection of photographs, tickets, souvenirs, etc. • Aluminium mesh • Strong scissors • Masking tape • Recycled paper pulp, dyed in 2–3 colours • 2–3 large rectangular plastic bowls • Couching cloths • Paper string or embroidery thread (floss) • Dowelling rod, 3mm (⅛in) diameter

4 Couch nine squares of one colour of pulp on to kitchen cloth, laying them in three rows of three squares (see Basic Techniques). Use the masking tape on the mesh as a guide for the spacing.

5 Cut 36 lengths of paper string or embroidery thread 6cm (2½in) long, to join the squares. Cut nine lengths 9cm (3½in) long, for the hanging loops. Arrange these on the paper squares.

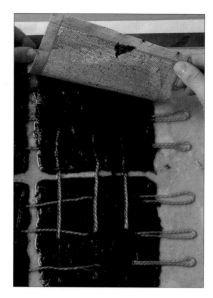

6 Lay nine more squares of the same coloured pulp on top of the first set, to hold the strings or threads in place.

7 Arrange your collection of materials on the squares of wet pulp.

8 Using a different-coloured pulp and the aluminium mesh as a mould, couch strips of pulp over the edges of the materials to hold them in place. Add extra colours at this stage, if desired. Leave the finished piece for several days to dry naturally. Thread the dowelling rod through the loops for hanging.

ACCORDION BOOK

This attractive little accordion book uses a folding technique developed in Japan to store long scrolls of paper. The cover paper is made by adding fragments of coloured silk and threads to the paper pulp before forming the sheets. Choose a ribbon to complement the colours in the paper you are using. You can tie the ribbons at one end to create a book, or undo both ends to display the accordion folds.

1 To make the covers, apply glue to one side of each piece of mount board. Place the board centrally on the wrong side of each piece of handmade paper.

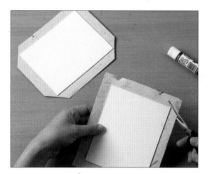

2 Cut across each corner of the two sheets of paper.

3 Fold the paper over the board and glue in place.

4 Using a craft knife and cutting mat, cut small slits in the centre of each long side on both covers, about 1cm (½in) in from the edge.

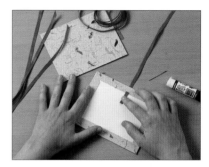

5 Cut four 25cm (10in) lengths of ribbon. Using a tapestry needle, push a piece of ribbon through each slit for about 2cm (¾in) and glue on to the inside of the board.

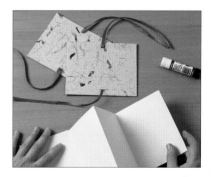

6 Divide the cartridge paper into eight equal sections. Fold along the length as shown.

▶

Materials and Equipment You Will Need
Paper glue • 2 pieces of mount (mat) board, 12 x 15cm (4¾ x 6in) • 2 sheets of handmade paper, 16 x 19cm (6¼ x 7½in) • Scissors • Craft (utility) knife • Cutting mat • Thin ribbon • Tapestry needle • Strip of cartridge (white construction) paper, 14 x 84cm (5½ x 33in)

7 Glue one end section of the accordion and place centrally on the inside of one cover. Repeat at the other end, making sure the two covers line up.

8 Tie one pair of ribbons to create a book with turning pages.

SPIRAL SWIRLS

In this decorative panel, handmade spirals are embedded in a thick pulp made from purple tissue paper. The spirals are made from painted paper and shiny foil, and are decorated with bright colours to give a very rich effect. This technique can also be used with beads or buttons, and natural materials such as shells and pebbles. Varnishing the inner edge of the mould prevents the pulp from sticking. In this project, nine spirals are arranged in three rows, but you can make as many shapes as you need to fit your mould and arrange them in a different pattern.

1 Fold long strips of painted paper and foil and wind each length round in a flat coil. Secure with coloured wire or thread then decorate with sealing wax. Make a number of different-sized spirals.

3 Using the tissue paper, make a coloured pulp (see Basic Techniques). Drain the pulp through a sieve to remove water and make a thicker pulp.

5 Leave the pulp in the frame to dry naturally, then carefully remove the pulp and spirals.

2 Varnish the inside of the frame. Place it mesh side down over a cloth laid on a flat surface. Arrange the spirals face down inside the frame.

4 Spoon the thick pulp over the spirals until the frame is completely filled. Using a small sponge, press the pulp gently to remove water.

6 Seal the piece with PVA glue, using a soft brush.

Materials and Equipment You Will Need

Painted paper • Aluminium foil • Thin coloured wire or coloured sewing threads (floss) • Sealing wax • Wood varnish • Decorator's brush, for applying varnish • Small frame or mould, with removable base • Couching cloth • Coloured tissue paper • Liquidizer • Sieve (strainer) • Plastic or glass bowl • Dessert spoon • Small sponge • PVA (white) glue • Brush, for applying glue

EMBROIDERED BIRD

This delightful bird was copied from a fragment of an old Indian skirt and it is embroidered, using a simple couching stitch, in a rich variety of threads. Black mica paint gives a slightly metallic effect, and the ormoline stops the gold metallic powder from tarnishing.

1 Fold two sheets of paper and tear them against a ruler to measure 16 x 16cm (6¼ x 6¼in) and 11 x 12cm (4¼ x 4¾in). Paint the first with blue paint mixed with water and black mica and the second with red paint mixed similarly. Leave to dry and iron between two sheets of tissue paper.

2 Trace the bird template at the back of the book. Transfer it on to the third piece of paper, using dressmaker's carbon paper. Cut out the bird shape.

3 Paint the bird with dark turquoise and rust paints. Wearing a face mask, apply gold powder mixed with ormoline.

4 Pin the red paper over the blue. Glue the bird in the centre and leave to dry. Using a face mask, paint the square and arch in gold powder with ormoline.

5 Cut a piece of backing fabric slightly smaller than the largest piece of paper and pin to the back. Couch dark-blue thread along the square and arch.

6 Remove the pins. Straight stitch the diamond patterns and borders, using different threads. Couch the outline of the bird in gold thread, then stitch tiny beads for its eye and crown. Add the spangles. Stitch the finished piece securely to the mount board, using a strong dark-blue thread.

Materials and Equipment You Will Need

3 sheets of handmade paper • Ruler • Artist's paintbrush • Blue, red, dark turquoise and rust acrylic paints • Black mica medium • Containers, for paints • Iron • 2 sheets of tissue paper • Pencil • Tracing paper • Dressmaker's carbon paper • Scissors • Face mask (respirator) • Gold metallic powder • Ormoline medium • Dressmaker's pins • PVA (white) glue • Brush, for glue • Vilene or backing fabric • Embroidery needles • Thick metallic gold embroidery thread (floss) • Embroidery threads (flosses), in dark blue, royal blue, red, dark turquoise and metallic gold • Small beads • Spangles • Mount (mat) board • Strong dark-blue thread

CONFETTI ALBUM

The handmade cover of this lovely album, designed for wedding photographs, is sprinkled with confetti. The paper for the pages needs to be quite thick to support the weight of the photographs. The spine and opening edges are covered with book cloth, available from specialist suppliers. If you have difficulty obtaining this, then make your own by gluing thin layout paper to light- or medium-weight fabric.

1 Decide on the size of the pages and covers for your album according to the size of the photographs. The pages need to be at least 5cm (2in) wider than required, to allow for the 'guards' which will accommodate the thickness of the photographs. Between 16–20 pages is an average number.

2 The handmade cover paper should be longer than the cover card, to allow for turnings. Using white pulp, make a sheet of paper (see Basic Techniques). While the sheet is draining over the vat, sprinkle confetti evenly over the surface.

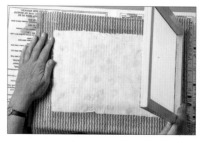

3 Couch the sheet on to cloths (see Basic Techniques). Make at least four confetti sheets to give you a choice. The extra sheets will be used to line the cover. Leave for several days to dry completely.

4 Using a craft knife and cutting mat, cut the pages to size. Make a light pencil mark at the top and bottom of each page, 2.5cm (1in) from the left-hand edge. Lay the ruler to touch both marks then score along this line with a bone folder or other straight edge. Fold upwards to make a 'guard'.

Materials and Equipment You Will Need

Thick handmade paper (see Basic Techniques) • Metal ruler • Thick cover cardboard • Mould and deckle • White recycled paper pulp • Large rectangular plastic bowl • Confetti • Couching cloths • Craft (utility) knife • Cutting mat • Pencil • Bone folder • Book cloth • PVA (white) glue • Brush, for applying glue • Scissors • Clamp • Hand drill or hole punch • White cord

5 Cut two pieces of cardboard for the covers, 1cm (½in) longer than the page height and 5mm (¼in) wider than their width. Cut a 2.5cm (1in) strip off both pieces and reserve.

7 Working on one cover at a time, take the reserved strip of cardboard and brush with glue. Place on the larger piece of book cloth, equidistant from the top and bottom and touching the marked line.

9 Take one of the smaller pieces of book cloth. Brush glue on the narrow edge and stick this edge to the opposite edge of the cover.

6 Cut two pieces of book cloth, 3cm (1¼in) longer than the covers and 9cm (3½in) wide. Cut two more pieces the same length and 2.5cm (1in) wide. On each piece, draw a line 1.5cm (⅝in) from one long side, to be turned in later.

8 Draw a line on the book cloth 3mm (⅛in) from the strip of card, on the side farthest away from the turn-in. Place the cloth wrong side up and brush with glue. Align the top and bottom edges with the strip of card. Glue the cover against the marked line.

10 Cut diagonally across all the corners of the cover, 5mm (¼in) from each corner. Place waste paper underneath then apply glue to the long turn-ins. Smoothing it with the bone folder, press the book cloth up, over the edge and down on the cardboard.

11 Press down the excess at the corners. Glue the remaining turn-ins and press carefully into place.

12 Cut another piece of book cloth a little shorter than the height of the cover, to go over the inside of the spine and overlap on to the cover, as on the outside. Glue it to the spine, down into the gap, then on to the cover, smoothing the cloth with the bone folder. Make the other cover to match.

DIAGRAM 1

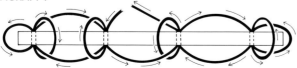

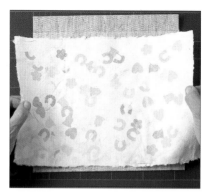

13 Use the best sheet of confetti paper for the front. If it is too wide, put a metal ruler on the paper and tear against the edge, creating another deckle. Trim the turn-ins to 1.5cm (⅝in) and glue down. Do the same for the back.

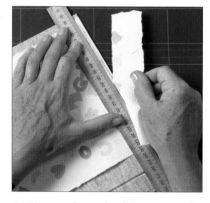

14 Measure the inside of the covers and tear two pieces of decorative paper which are slightly smaller all round. Glue one inside each cover, using the bone folder over a piece of clean paper to ensure the paper is stuck at the edges.

15 To assemble the album, stack all the pages and sandwich them between the covers. Take a strip of cardboard the same size as the spine and lay it on top then clamp the album together. Make evenly spaced marks along the centre of the cardboard strip then drill holes at these points. The larger the album, the more holes will be needed. You can use a hole punch, but you will need to punch each sheet separately.

16 Discard the cardboard strip. Cut a length of cord and thread through the holes in the spine to hold the album together (see Diagram 1). Tie the ends securely together, fray and fluff them out and trim neatly.

TEMPLATES

If the templates need to be enlarged, either use a grid system or a photocopier. For the grid system, trace the template and draw a grid of evenly spaced squares over your tracing. To scale up, draw a large grid on to another piece of paper. Copy the outline on to the second square, taking each square individually and drawing the relevant part of the outline in the larger square. Finally, draw over the lines to make sure they are continuous. Alternatively, two different sizes of graph paper may be used.

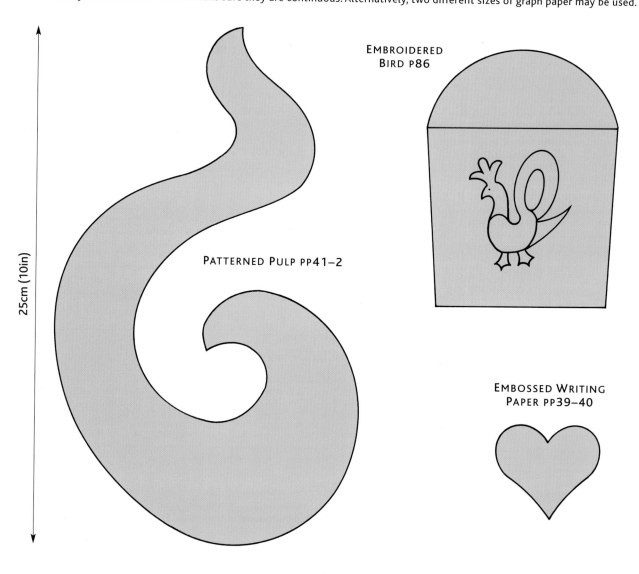

EMBROIDERED
BIRD P86

25cm (10in)

PATTERNED PULP PP41–2

EMBOSSED WRITING
PAPER PP39–40

24¹/₂cm (9³/₄in)

EMBOSSED WRITING PAPER PP39–40

Enlarge on a photocopier or scanner to obtain required size.

Notepaper Case p54

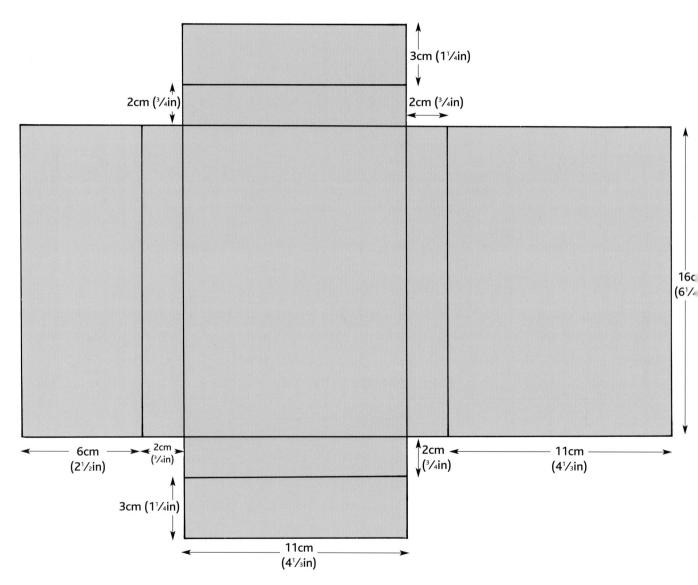

3cm (1¼in)

2cm (¾in)

2cm (¾in)

16c
(6½

6cm
(2½in)

2cm
(¾in)

2cm
(¾in)

11cm
(4⅓in)

3cm (1¼in)

11cm
(4⅓in)

Suppliers and Acknowledgements

Most good craft stores should be able to supply the materials required for the projects in this book. Listed here are a few of the major stores, as well as more specialist suppliers used by the author.

UK
Falkiner Fine Papers
76 Southampton Row,
London
NWC1B 4AR
Tel: 020 7831 1151
www.falkiners.com

Maureen Richardson
(handmade papers)
Romilly,
Brilley,
Hay-on-Wye,
Hereford
HR3 6HE

Paperchase
Numerous stores nationwide
www.paperchase.co.uk

Pulp and Paper
   Information Centre
1 Rivenhall Road,
Westlea, Swindon,
Wiltshire
SN5 7BE
Tel: 01793 889 615
www.ppic.org.uk

USA
Pearl Paint Co.
308 Canal Street,
New York,
NY 10013
Tel: 1-800-451-7327
www.pearlpaint.com

Fascinating Folds
P.O. Box 10070,
Glendale,
AZ 85318
Tel: 602-375-9978
www.fascinating-folds.com

Gold's Artworks Inc.
2100 North Pine Street,
Lumberton,
NC 28318
Tel: 910-739-9605
www.goldcottonlinterpulp.com

Kate's Paperie
561 Broadway,
New York,
NY 10012
Tel: 1-800-809-9880
www.katepaperie.com

Twinrocker Handmade Paper
100 East 3rd Street,
Brookston,
IN 47923
Tel: 765-563-3119
www.twinrocker.com

Australia
Lincraft
Stores nationwide
lincraft.com.au

Spotlight
Stores nationwide
www.spotlight.com.au

Peterkin Premium
   Paper Merchant
12A Harold Street,
Dianella 6059,
Western Australia
Tel: 08-9271-9255
www.peterkin.com.au

Quire Handmade Paper
PO Box 248,
Belair 5052,
Adelaide, South Australia
Tel: 08-8295-2966

Artwise Amazing Paper
186 Enmore Road,
Enmore 2042,
Sydney, New South Wales
Tel: 02-9519-8237
www.amazingpaper.com.au

AUTHOR'S ACKNOWLEDGEMENTS
The publishers and author would like to thank all those who helped compile this book, particularly the project contributors: Lindsay Bloxam, pages 47 and 65; Wendy Carlton-Dewhirst, pages 27, 44 and 51; Brenda Connor, pages 67 and 86; Vivien Frank, pages 39 and 89; Nicola Jackson, pages 54 and 75; Anne Johnson, pages 25, 33 and 79; and Jenny Nutbeem, pages 30, 69 and 81.

Also to the artists who contributed work to the Gallery section: Lindsay Bloxam, Wendy Carlton-Dewhirst, Elizabeth Couzins-Scott, Susan Cutts, Carol Farrow, Anne Johnson and David Watson.

Thank you to Peter Williams and Georgina Rhodes, the photographer and stylist, for their inspired project shots. Also to Rodney Forte, for his flexibility and good humour when shooting the step-by-step sequences.

INDEX